"It's hard to connect with your child without first understanding where they are. As counselors and speakers at parenting events across the country, we spend a great deal of time teaching parents about development. To know *where* your child is—not just physically, but emotionally, socially, and spiritually, helps you to truly know and understand *who* your child is. And that understanding is the key to connecting. The Phase Guides give you the tools to do just that. Our wise friends Reggie and Kristen have put together an insightful, hopeful, practical, and literal year-by-year guide that will help you to understand and connect with your child at every age."

SISSY GOFF
M.ED., LPC-MHSP, DIRECTOR OF CHILD & ADOLESCENT COUNSELING AT DAYSTAR COUNSELING MINISTRIES IN NASHVILLE, TENNESSEE, SPEAKER AND AUTHOR OF ARE MY KIDS ON TRACK?

"These resources for parents are fantastically empowering, absolute in their simplicity, and completely doable in every way. The hard work that has gone into the Phase Project will echo through the next generation of children in powerful ways."

JENNIFER WALKER
RN BSN, AUTHOR AND FOUNDER OF MOMS ON CALL

"We all know where we want to end up in our parenting, but how to get there can seem like an unsolved mystery. Through the Phase Project series, Reggie Joiner and Kristen Ivy team up to help us out. The result is a resource that guides us through the different seasons of raising children, and provides a road map to parenting in such a way that we finish up with very few regrets."

SANDRA STANLEY
FOSTER CARE ADVOCATE, BLOGGER, WIFE TO ANDY STANLEY, MOTHER OF THREE

"Not only are the Phase Guides the most creative and well-thought-out guides to parenting I have ever encountered, these books are ESSENTIAL to my daily parenting. With a 13-year-old, 11-year-old, and 9-year-old at home, I am swimming in their wake of daily drama and delicacy. These books are a reminder to enjoy every second. Because it's just a phase."

CARLOS WHITTAKER
AUTHOR, SPEAKER, FATHER OF THREE

"As the founder of Minnie's Food Pantry, I see thousands of people each month with children who will benefit from the advice, guidance, and nuggets of information on how to celebrate and understand the phases of their child's life. Too often we feel like we're losing our mind when sweet little Johnny starts to change his behavior into a person we do not know. I can't wait to start implementing the principles of these books with my clients to remind them . . . it's just a phase."

CHERYL JACKSON
*FOUNDER OF MINNIE'S FOOD PANTRY, AWARD-W
AND GRANDMOTHER*

D0916420

"I began exploring this resource with my counselor hat on, thinking how valuable this will be for the many parents I spend time with in my office. I ended up taking my counselor hat off and putting on my parent hat. Then I kept thinking about friends who are teachers, coaches, youth pastors, and children's ministers, who would want this in their hands. What a valuable resource the Orange team has given us to better understand and care for the kids and adolescents we love. I look forward to sharing it broadly."

DAVID THOMAS
LMSW, DIRECTOR OF FAMILY COUNSELING, DAYSTAR COUNSELING MINISTRIES, SPEAKER AND AUTHOR OF ARE MY KIDS ON TRACK? AND WILD THINGS: THE ART OF NURTURING BOYS

"I have always wished someone would hand me a manual for parenting. Well, the Phase Guides are more than what I wished for. They guide, inspire, and challenge me as a parent—while giving me incredible insight into my children at each age and phase. Our family will be using these every year!"

COURTNEY DEFEO
AUTHOR OF IN THIS HOUSE, WE WILL GIGGLE, MOTHER OF TWO

"As I speak to high school students and their parents, I always wonder to myself: What would it have been like if they had better seen what was coming next? What if they had a guide that would tell them what to expect and how to be ready? What if they could anticipate what is predictable about the high school years before they actually hit? These Phase Guides give a parent that kind of preparation so they can have a plan when they need it most."

JOSH SHIPP
AUTHOR, TEEN EXPERT, AND YOUTH SPEAKER

"The Phase Guides are incredibly creative, well researched, and filled with inspirational actions for everyday life. Each age-specific guide is catalytic for equipping parents to lead and love their kids as they grow up. I'm blown away and deeply encouraged by the content and by its creators. I highly recommend Phase resources for all parents, teachers, and influencers of children. This is the stuff that challenges us and changes our world. Get them. Read them. And use them!"

DANIELLE STRICKLAND
OFFICER WITH THE SALVATION ARMY, AUTHOR, SPEAKER, MOTHER OF TWO

"It's true that parenting is one of life's greatest joys but it is not without its challenges. If we're honest, parenting can sometimes feel like trying to choreograph a dance to an ever-changing beat. It can be clumsy and riddled with well-meaning missteps. If parenting is a dance, this Parenting Guide is a skilled instructor refining your technique and helping you move gracefully to a steady beat. For those of us who love to plan ahead, this guide will help you anticipate what's to come so you can be poised and ready to embrace the moments you want to enjoy."

TINA NAIDOO
MSSW, LCSW EXECUTIVE DIRECTOR, THE POTTER'S HOUSE OF DALLAS, INC.

PARENTING YOUR ONE-YEAR-OLD

A GUIDE TO MAKING THE MOST OF THE "I CAN DO IT" PHASE

KRISTEN IVY AND REGGIE JOINER

PARENTING YOUR ONE-YEAR-OLD
A GUIDE TO MAKING THE MOST OF THE
"I CAN DO IT" PHASE

Published by Orange, a division of The reThink Group, Inc.,
5870 Charlotte Lane, Suite 300,
Cumming, GA 30040 U.S.A.

©2017 The Phase Project
Authors: Kristen Ivy and Reggie Joiner
Lead Editor: Karen Wilson
Editing Team: Melanie Williams, Hannah Crosby, Sherry Surratt

Art Direction: Ryan Boon and Hannah Crosby
Book Design: FiveStone and Sharon van Rossum
Project Manager : Nate Brandt

Printed in the United States of America
First Edition 2017

16 17 18 19 20 21 22 23 24 25

09/2021

Special thanks to:

Jim Burns, Ph.D for guidance and consultation on having conversations about sexual integrity

Jon Acuff for guidance and consultation on having conversations about technological responsibility

Jean Sumner, MD for guidance and consultation on having conversations about healthy habits

Every educator, counselor, community leader, and researcher who invested in the Phase Project

TABLE OF CONTENTS

HOW TO USE THIS ~~BOOK~~ ~~JOURNAL~~ GUIDE

The guide you hold in your hand doesn't have very many words, but it does have a lot of ideas. Some of these ideas come from thousands of hours of research. Others come from parents, educators, and volunteers who spend every day with kids the same age as yours. This guide won't tell you everything about your kid, but it will tell you a few things about kids at this age.

The best way to use this guide is to take what these pages tell you about toddlers and combine it with what you know is true about your toddler.

Let's sum it up:

THINGS ABOUT TODDLERS +

THOUGHTS ABOUT *YOUR* TODDLER =

YOUR GUIDE TO THE NEXT 52 WEEKS OF PARENTING

After each idea in this guide, there are pages with a few questions designed to prompt you to think about your kid, your family, and yourself as a parent. The only guarantee we give to parents who use this guide is this: You will mess up some things as a parent this year. Actually, that's a guarantee to every parent, regardless. But you, you picked up this book! You want to be a better parent. And that's what we hope this guide will do: help you parent your toddler just a little better, simply because you paused to consider a few ideas that can help you make the most of this phase.

THE ONE-YEAR-OLD PHASE

I'm not sure what captivates me more . . . the spontaneous belly laugh or the drool-mouthed wonder on their angelic faces. I can fall in love with a one-year-old faster than they can stink up a room with a saggy diaper. The cherub cheeks and adorably fat thighs draw me in, almost enough to make me overlook their incessantly snotty nose and the jelly they just smeared in their wispy new-grown hair. Almost.

It's the mess that gets me. Their little fingers are drawn like magnets to anything they can break or mangle. The moment their hands become sticky-gooey, an internal signal screams somewhere in their little bodies, "Wipe yourself on something clean and white. Right now!"

Sitting at the dinner table, I see the same look on my granddaughter Mollie's face that I saw on her daddy's face so many years ago. It's the look of curiosity that drives a toddler to snatch and smear, squish, then shriek with delight. I glance across to see the look on her mom's face. It reads: *Could I just eat a meal without being completely grossed out, maybe while the food is still reasonably warm?*

It's hard to believe, but yes, that day will come. But not until Mollie has discovered how much pasta her ears will hold or what a bowl of applesauce feels like as it drips down her face, neck, and eventually . . . to the floor.

Sweet discovery is what this phase is made of. It's what makes patience and endurance such prized commodities for the parents of this age. You are helping your one-year-old navigate the mess of discovery.

During this phase, your brilliant bundle of exhaustless energy will climb her first stairs, say her first sentence, and begin to test her independence—independence that will be illustrated with piercing shrieks, and that vehemently spoken word: "No!"

But within the mess is an indescribable joy. He just toddled his first Frankenstein steps, three in a row, boasting the proud look of an astronaut landing on the moon. She just grabbed a crayon and scribbled her first work of art. Your darling can identify his nose and eyes and ears on command (to rousing applause), and you are certain he has the makings of a brain surgeon.

Sweet joy and pride so big it hurts—this is what wells up in the hearts of moms and dads as they watch their one-year-old develop into a little person with opinions and intellect and personality. And as you gaze, you begin to realize what this really means. Not only do you get a ringside seat to watch the beauty of potential form right before your eyes, but you get the joy of helping influence, train, and build who your child will become. Just remember: There will come a day when your once-helpless baby will bathe, dress, and feed himself, but the journey to get there comes with a little mess along the way.

- SHERRY SURRATT
FORMER PRESIDENT AND CEO OF MOPS INTERNATIONAL, SPEAKER, AUTHOR, & GRANDMOTHER

52
WEEKS
—
TO PARENT YOUR
ONE-YEAR-OLD

WHEN YOU SEE
HOW MUCH

Time

YOU HAVE LEFT

——

YOU TEND TO DO

More

WITH THE TIME
YOU HAVE NOW.

THERE ARE APPROXIMATELY

936 WEEKS

FROM THE TIME A BABY IS BORN UNTIL THEY GROW UP AND MOVE TO WHATEVER IS NEXT.

It may seem hard to believe, but at least 52 of those weeks have already passed you by. And, while the future still feels far away, you're probably beginning to realize that your baby is growing up faster than you ever dreamed.

That's why every week counts. Of course, each week on its own might not feel significant. There may be weeks this year when you feel like all you've accomplished was translating toddler babble. That's okay.

Take a deep breath.
You don't have to get everything done this week.

But what happens in your child's life week after week, year after year, adds up over time. So, it might be a good idea to put a number to your weeks.

MEASURE IT OUT.

Write down the number of weeks that have already passed since your toddler was born. Then write down the number of weeks you have left before they graduate high school.

HINT: If you want a little help counting it out, you can download the free Parent Cue app on all mobile platforms.

_____

_____

_____

CREATE A VISUAL COUNTDOWN.

Find a jar and fill it with one marble for each week you have remaining with your child. Then make a habit of removing one marble every week as a reminder to make the most of your time you have with your child.

Where can you place your visual countdown so you will see it frequently?

_____

_____

_____

_____

Which day of the week is best for you to remove a marble?

_____

_____

_____

Is there anything you want to do each week as you remove
a marble? *(Examples: say a prayer, write in a baby book, retell
one favorite memory from this past week)*

_____

_____

_____

_____

_____

_____

_____

_____

_____

_____

_____

EVERY PHASE IS A
TIMEFRAME
IN A KID'S LIFE
WHEN YOU CAN
LEVERAGE
DISTINCTIVE
OPPORTUNITIES
TO INFLUENCE
THEIR

future.

YOU ONLY HAVE

52 WEEKS

WITH YOUR ONE-YEAR-OLD

while they are still one.

Then they will be two,

and you will never know them as a one-year-old again.

That might be incredibly emotional,

or it might be the best news you've heard all day.

Or to say it another way:

Before you know it, your toddler will grow up a little more and . . .

be potty trained.

speak in sentences.

dress themselves.

Just remember, the phase you are in now has remarkable potential. Before their second birthday, there are some distinctive opportunities you don't want to miss. So, as you count down the next 52 weeks, pay attention to what makes these weeks different from the rest of the weeks you will have with your child as they grow.

What are some things you have noticed about your one-year-old in this phase that you really enjoy?

_____

_____

_____

_____

_____

_____

_____

_____

_____

_____

_____

_____

_____

_____

_____

_____

_____

_____

What is something new you are learning as a parent during this phase?

_____

_____

_____

_____

_____

_____

_____

_____

_____

_____

_____

_____

_____

_____

_____

_____

_____

_____

_____

ONE

—

THE PHASE WHEN
NOBODY'S ON TIME,
EVERYTHING'S A
MESS, AND ONE
EAGER TODDLER
WILL INSIST,

"I can do it."

EXPECT TO BE LATE.

Maybe you had to wait for your toddler to "do it myself" (just try and stop them). Or maybe they impressively filled a clean diaper just as you got into the car. Whatever the reason, this phase will make even the most punctual adult miss the mark occasionally.

LOOK FORWARD TO A FEW FASHION STATEMENTS.

Expect a few mismatched outfits, magic marker tattoos, sticker collages, and other various states of creative expression. In this phase, you will choose not only your battles, but also which messes will just have to be tolerated.

THEIR STRUGGLE FOR INDEPENDENCE HAS BEGUN.

You feel it the first time they try to feed themselves and dump applesauce down the front of their shirt. Just remember, by letting them do some things "myself," they're not only learning new skills, they're also developing the confidence they need in order to move to the next phase.

YOUR

ONE-

YEAR-

OLD

IS

changing.

PHYSICALLY

- Starts to walk (12-15 months)
- Walks backwards and sideways (15-18 months)
- Scribbles with crayons (15-18 months)
- Climbs up and down stairs; jumps in place (18-24 months)

VERBALLY

- Points to objects when you name them (18 months)
- Says 10-20 words, mostly nouns and pronouns (18 months)
- Says 40-50 words and forms two-word sentences (24 months)
- Understands more than they can communicate

MENTALLY

- Follows simple instructions
- Benefits from repetition
- Learns through engaging their five senses

EMOTIONALLY

- Recognizes basic emotions in others
- Has trouble sharing
- May begin role-play activities
- Displays separation anxiety
- Plays next to, rather than with, playmates

What are some changes you are noticing in your one-year-old?

_____

_____

_____

_____

_____

_____

_____

You may disagree with some of the characteristics we've shared about one-year-olds. That's because every one-year-old is unique. What makes your one-year-old different from one-year-olds in general?

_____

_____

_____

_____

_____

_____

_____

_____

What do you want to remember about this year with your one-year-old?

Mark this page. Throughout the year, write down a few simple things you want to remember. If you want to be really thorough, there are about 52 blank lines. But some weeks, you may choose to baby-proof the cabinets instead of writing down a memory. That's okay.

_____

_____

_____

_____

_____

_____

_____

_____

_____

_____

_____

_____

_____

_____

_____

_____

_____

_____

_____

_____

_____

_____

_____

_____

_____

_____

_____

_____

_____

_____

_____

_____

_____

_____

_____

_____

_____

_____

_____

_____

_____

_____

_____

_____

_____

_____

_____

_____

_____

_____

_____

_____

_____

_____

_____

_____

_____

_____

_____

_____

SIX
THINGS

—

EVERY KID
NEEDS

YOUR KID NEEDS 6 THINGS OVER TIME

LOVE

STORIES

WORDS

WORK

TRIBES

FUN

OVER THE NEXT 884 WEEKS, YOUR CHILD WILL NEED MANY THINGS.

Some of the things your kid needs will change from phase to phase, but there are six things that every kid needs at every phase. In fact, these things may be the most important things you give your kid—other than food. Kids need food.

EVERY KID, AT EVERY PHASE, NEEDS . . .

LOVE
to give them a sense of WORTH.

STORIES
to give them a bigger PERSPECTIVE.

WORK
to give them SIGNIFICANCE.

FUN
to give them CONNECTION.

TRIBES
to give them BELONGING.

WORDS
to give them DIRECTION.

The next few pages are designed to help you think about how you can give these things to your one-year-old—before they turn two.

EVERY KID

NEEDS

love

OVER TIME

—

TO GIVE THEM

A SENSE OF

worth.

ONE QUESTION YOUR ONE-YEAR-OLD IS ASKING

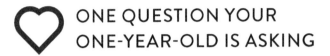

Your toddler's changing ability is a crisis—for you, and for them. This is a season filled with uncertainty, imperfection, and even failure as they struggle to keep up with all their newly developing skills.

Your one-year-old is asking one major question:

"AM I ABLE?"

As the parent of a one-year-old who may scream more than you imagined, sleep less than you had hoped, or make more messes than you thought possible, you may feel overwhelmed at times. But remember this—in order to give your one-year-old the love they need, you only need to do one thing:

EMBRACE their physical needs.

When you embrace your toddler's physical needs, you . . .
communicate that they are safe,
establish that the world can be trusted,
and demonstrate that they are worth loving.

You are probably doing more than you realize to show your one-year-old just how much you love them. Make a list of the ways you already show up consistently to embrace your toddler's physical needs.

You may need to look at this list on a bad day to remember what a great parent you are.

Showing love requires paying attention to what someone likes. What does your toddler seem to enjoy the most right now?

It's impossible to love anyone with the relentless effort a one-year-old demands unless you have a little time for yourself. What can you do to refuel each week so you are able to give your toddler the love they need?

_____

_____

_____

_____

_____

_____

_____

_____

_____

_____

_____

_____

_____

_____

_____

_____

_____

Who do you have around you supporting you this year?

_____

_____

_____

_____

_____

_____

_____

_____

_____

_____

_____

_____

_____

_____

_____

_____

_____

_____

_____

_____

_____

_____

EVERY KID

NEEDS

stories

OVER TIME

—

TO GIVE THEM

A BIGGER

perspective.

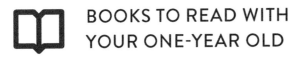

BOOKS TO READ WITH YOUR ONE-YEAR OLD

INSIDE OUT UPSIDE DOWN
by Stan and Jan Berenstain

BLUE HAT, GREEN HAT
by Sandra Boynton

OPPOSITES
by Sandra Boynton

THE RUNAWAY BUNNY
by Margaret Wise Brown

FIVE LITTLE MONKEYS JUMPING ON THE BED
by Eileen Christelow

FREIGHT TRAIN
by Donald Crews

CLICK, CLACK, MOO COWS THAT TYPE
by Doreen Cronin

LLAMA, LLAMA (SERIES)
by Anna Dewdney

WHISTLE FOR WILLIE
by Ezra Jack Keats

ARE YOU MY MOTHER?
by P.D. Eastman

GO, DOG. GO!
by P.D. Eastman

GOODNIGHT, GOODNIGHT, CONSTRUCTION SITE
by Sheri Duskey Rinker

LITTLE BLUE TRUCK
by Alice Schertle

THE FOOT BOOK
by Dr. Seuss

MR. BROWN CAN MOO! CAN YOU?
by Dr. Seuss

DUCK ON A BIKE
by David Shannon

SHEEP IN A JEEP
by Nancy E. Shaw

CAPS FOR SALE
by Esphyr Slobodkina

Kids need the kind of stories you will read to them over time. But they also need family stories. What can you do this year to capture your family's story so you can retell the story of this year to your child when they are older?

_____

_____

_____

_____

_____

_____

_____

_____

_____

_____

_____

_____

_____

_____

_____

_____

_____

_____

What makes your family history unique? How can you preserve
the story of your family's history for your child?

_____

_____

_____

_____

_____

_____

_____

_____

_____

_____

_____

_____

_____

_____

_____

_____

_____

_____

_____

Are there other stories that matter to you? What are they, and how will you share those stories with your toddler?

_____

_____

_____

_____

_____

_____

_____

_____

_____

_____

_____

_____

_____

_____

_____

_____

_____

_____

_____

EVERY KID

NEEDS

work

OVER TIME

—

TO GIVE

THEM

significance.

WORK YOUR
ONE-YEAR-OLD CAN DO

WALK

**PICK UP A TOY AND
PUT IT AWAY**

HOLD A SIPPY CUP

DRINK FROM A STRAW

**TAKE TRASH TO
THE TRASH CAN**

**FOLLOW ONE-STEP
INSTRUCTIONS**
(like, "Hand it to me.")

**HELP FILL A
PET'S FOOD DISH**

FEED THEMSELVES

**HELP AS YOU
DRESS THEM**
(by not running away)

UNDRESS THEMSELVES

CLEAN UP SPILLS
(or spread the water around
on the floor)

What are some things your one-year-old has worked to accomplish so far?

Letting your toddler "do it myself" takes patience—and a lot of wet wipes. How are you allowing for extra time for your toddler to try new things? What do you do to reward their efforts?

_____

_____

_____

_____

_____

_____

_____

_____

_____

_____

_____

_____

_____

_____

_____

_____

_____

_____

What are some things you hope your toddler will be able to do independently in the next phase? How are you helping them develop those skills now?

_____

_____

_____

_____

_____

_____

_____

_____

_____

_____

_____

_____

_____

_____

_____

_____

_____

_____

EVERY KID

NEEDS

fun

OVER TIME

—

TO GIVE

THEM

connection.

WAYS TO HAVE FUN WITH YOUR ONE-YEAR-OLD

TOYS:

TRUCKS, TRAINS, AND DOLLS
(12 months+)

SHAPE SORTERS
(12-18 months)

STACKING RINGS
(12-18 months)

PUSH TOYS
(12-18 months)

JUMBO CRAYONS
(15 months)

A SOFT BALL FOR ROLLING AND THROWING
(16 months)

PEG PUZZLES
(18-24 months)

POUNDING BENCH
(18-24 months)

BIG BLOCKS
(24 months)

ANYTHING WITH A MIRROR
(4 months-forever)
(but maybe not the glass kind unless it's anchored to a wall)

ACTIVITIES:

GO TO THE PARK

SING "ITSY-BITSY-SPIDER"

BLOW BUBBLES

PUSH A SWING

ROLL A BALL

DO A SILLY DANCE

PLAY "PEEK-A-BOO"

What are some activities that make you and your
one-year-old laugh?

_____

_____

_____

_____

_____

_____

_____

_____

_____

_____

_____

_____

_____

_____

_____

_____

_____

_____

When are the best times of the day, or week, for you to set aside to have fun with your one-year-old?

_____

_____

_____

_____

_____

_____

_____

_____

_____

_____

_____

_____

_____

_____

_____

_____

_____

_____

_____

_____

_____

What are some ways you want to celebrate the special days coming up this year?

2ND BIRTHDAY

HOLIDAYS

EVERY KID

NEEDS

tribes

OVER TIME

—

TO GIVE

THEM

belonging.

ADULTS WHO MIGHT INFLUENCE YOUR ONE-YEAR-OLD

PARENTS

PARENT'S FRIENDS

GRANDPARENTS

NURSERY WORKERS

AUNTS AND UNCLES

BABYSITTERS OR NANNIES

List at least five adults who have influence in your one-year-old's life right now.

🔑 HINT: They're probably the adults your one-year-old reaches for and doesn't shy away from.

_____

_____

_____

_____

_____

_____

_____

_____

_____

_____

_____

_____

_____

_____

_____

What is one way these adults could help you and your toddler this year?

EXAMPLES: pray for you, read to your toddler, take your toddler to the park

_____

_____

_____

_____

_____

_____

_____

_____

_____

_____

_____

_____

_____

_____

_____

_____

What are a few ways you could show these adults appreciation for the significant role they play in your child's life?

_____

_____

_____

_____

_____

_____

_____

_____

_____

_____

_____

_____

_____

_____

_____

_____

_____

_____

_____

_____

EVERY KID

NEEDS

words

OVER TIME

—

TO GIVE

THEM

direction.

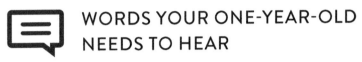

WORDS YOUR ONE-YEAR-OLD NEEDS TO HEAR

Improving your child's vocabulary will help them in the phases to come. Here are a few ways you can help:

1.

Talk to your toddler—the more, the better.

2.

Repeat what they say, and add words. (When they say "truck," you say, "Would you like to play with your truck?")

3.

Make eye contact.

4.

Point at objects when you name them.

What word (or words) describe your hopes for your child in this phase?

DETERMINED	MOTIVATED	GENTLE
ENCOURAGING	INTROSPECTIVE	PASSIONATE
SELF-ASSURED	ENTHUSIASTIC	PATIENT
ASSERTIVE	JOYFUL	FORGIVING
DARING	ENTERTAINING	CREATIVE
INSIGHTFUL	INDEPENDENT	WITTY
COMPASSIONATE	OBSERVANT	AMBITIOUS
AMIABLE	SENSITIVE	HELPFUL
EASY-GOING	ENDEARING	AUTHENTIC
DILIGENT	ADVENTUROUS	INVENTIVE
PROACTIVE	HONEST	DEVOTED
OPTIMISTIC	CURIOUS	GENUINE
FEARLESS	DEPENDABLE	ATTENTIVE
AFFECTIONATE	GENEROUS	HARMONIOUS
COURAGEOUS	COMMITTED	EMPATHETIC
CAUTIOUS	RESPONSIBLE	COURAGEOUS
DEVOTED	TRUSTWORTHY	FLEXIBLE
INQUISITIVE	THOUGHTFUL	CAREFUL
PATIENT	LOYAL	NURTURING
OPEN-MINDED	KIND	RELIABLE

Where can you place those words in your home so they will remind you what you want for your child this year?

_____

_____

_____

_____

_____

_____

_____

_____

_____

_____

_____

_____

_____

_____

_____

_____

_____

_____

_____

One-year-olds may say up to 50 words before their second birthday. Write down some of your toddler's first and favorite words. *(At some point this year, try to get a recording of their voice—it will have changed before you know it.)*

FOUR CONVERSATIONS

—

TO HAVE IN THIS PHASE

WHEN YOU KNOW
WHERE YOU WANT
TO GO,

AND YOU KNOW
WHERE YOU ARE
NOW,

YOU CAN ALWAYS
DO SOMETHING

TO MOVE IN A
BETTER DIRECTION.

→

OVER THE NEXT 884 WEEKS OF YOUR CHILD'S LIFE, SOME CONVERSATIONS MAY MATTER MORE THAN OTHERS.

WHAT YOU SAY, FOR EXAMPLE, REGARDING . . .	MIGHT HAVE LESS IMPACT ON THEIR FUTURE THAN WHAT YOU SAY REGARDING . . .
Pirates	Health
Spiders	Sex
and Football	Technology
	or Faith.

The next pages are about the conversations that matter most. On the left page is a destination—what you might want to be true in your kid's life 884 weeks from now. On the right page is a goal for conversations with your one-year-old and a few suggestions about what you might want to say.

Healthy habits

—

LEARNING TO STRENGTHEN MY BODY THROUGH EXERCISE, NUTRITION, AND SELF-ADVOCACY

THIS YEAR YOU WILL

ESTABLISH BASIC NUTRITION

SO YOUR CHILD WILL HAVE CONSISTENT CARE AND EXPERIENCE A VARIETY OF FOOD.

Your one-year-old understands the world better when you talk about what you're doing as you do it. So build a foundation for healthy habits by repeating a few simple phrases this year . . .

SAY THINGS LIKE . . .

TODAY, WE'RE GOING TO SEE DOCTOR MARK.
(Prioritize well visits with your pediatrician at 12, 15, 18, and 24 months.)

IT'S NAP TIME.

LET'S GO OUTSIDE.

YUM! IT'S GREEN BEANS!

LET'S WASH YOUR HANDS.

What are your goals for providing your one-year-old with good nutrition and exercise? *(Okay, "exercise" may be a stretch, but running after big kids at the park counts.)*

_____

_____

_____

_____

_____

_____

_____

_____

_____

_____

_____

_____

_____

_____

_____

_____

_____

_____

_____

Who will help you monitor and improve your one-year-old's health this year?

_____

_____

_____

_____

_____

_____

_____

_____

_____

_____

_____

_____

_____

_____

_____

_____

_____

_____

_____

_____

What are your own health goals for this year? How can you improve the habits in your own life—*even in a phase when your most common health question might be, "Should I use their nap time to sleep or shower or eat?"*

_____

_____

_____

_____

_____

_____

_____

_____

_____

_____

_____

_____

_____

_____

_____

_____

_____

_____

_____

_____

_____

_____

_____

_____

_____

_____

_____

_____

_____

_____

_____

_____

_____

_____

_____

_____

_____

_____

_____

_____

_____

_____

_____

_____

Sexual integrity

—

GUARDING MY
POTENTIAL FOR
INTIMACY THROUGH
APPROPRIATE
BOUNDARIES
AND MUTUAL
RESPECT

THIS YEAR YOU WILL

INTRODUCE THEM TO THEIR BODY

SO YOUR CHILD WILL DISCOVER THEIR BODY
AND DEFINE PRIVACY.

Your conversations with your child regarding sexual integrity will never be simpler than they are right now. But it's never too early to start with some of the right words.

SAY THINGS LIKE . . .

WHERE'S YOUR BELLY BUTTON?

THERE'S YOUR NOSE.

THAT'S YOUR
VAGINA / PENIS.

(Help your child learn the correct names of body parts—experts suggest that learning proper words can protect your kid from potential harm as well as create a positive view of their body.)

What influences shaped your views of sex growing up? *(parents, media, friends, other adults . . .)*

_____

_____

_____

_____

_____

_____

_____

_____

_____

_____

_____

_____

_____

_____

_____

_____

_____

_____

_____

_____

How does your own life story shape your future hopes for your child in this area?

_____

_____

_____

_____

_____

_____

_____

_____

_____

_____

_____

_____

_____

_____

_____

_____

_____

_____

_____

_____

_____

_____

When it comes to your child's sexuality, what do you hope is true for them 884 weeks from now?

_____

_____

_____

_____

_____

_____

_____

_____

_____

_____

_____

_____

_____

_____

_____

_____

_____

_____

_____

_____

_____

Are you and your spouse, or your child's other parent, on the
same page when it comes to talking about sex with your child?
How might you work on a plan to communicate your
hopes, expectations, and real-time conversations with your
child about sex?

_____

_____

_____

_____

_____

_____

_____

_____

_____

_____

_____

_____

_____

_____

_____

Technological responsibility

—

LEVERAGING THE
POTENTIAL OF ONLINE
EXPERIENCES TO
ENHANCE MY OFFLINE
COMMUNITY
AND SUCCESS

THIS YEAR YOU WILL

ENJOY THE ADVANTAGES

SO YOUR CHILD WILL EXPERIENCE BOUNDARIES
AND HAVE POSITIVE EXPOSURE.

Every one-year-old is eager to discover the magical screen with lights and buttons. Even though there's definitely such a thing as too much screen time, technology does have a few benefits for you and your one-year-old. So start having a few conversations about the digital devices in your home.

SAY THINGS LIKE . . .

NO JUICE BY THE COMPUTER.

**TABLETS DON'T
GO IN THE BATHTUB.**

A PHONE IS NOT A HAMMER.

**LET'S TURN
OFF THE TV NOW.**
(One-year-olds don't need
to watch a full season of
Sesame Street in one sitting.)

LOOK AT YOU!
(Take as many photos as you like.
You will enjoy seeing them later.)

What kind of digital access was available to you when you were growing up? How have things changed since then?

_____

_____

_____

_____

_____

_____

_____

_____

_____

_____

_____

_____

_____

_____

_____

_____

_____

_____

_____

_____

What are some issues you think may come up as you raise your child in a digitally connected world? Where can you go to find advice to help navigate those issues?

_____

_____

_____

_____

_____

_____

_____

_____

_____

_____

_____

_____

_____

_____

_____

_____

_____

_____

When it comes to your child's engagement with technology, what do you hope is true for them 884 weeks from now?

_____

_____

_____

_____

_____

_____

_____

_____

_____

_____

_____

_____

_____

_____

_____

_____

_____

_____

_____

What are your own personal values and disciplines when it comes to leveraging technology? Are there ways you want to improve your own savvy, skill, or responsibility in this area?

_____

_____

_____

_____

_____

_____

_____

_____

_____

_____

_____

_____

_____

_____

_____

_____

_____

_____

_____

Authentic faith

—

TRUSTING JESUS
IN A WAY THAT
TRANSFORMS HOW
I LOVE GOD,
MYSELF,
AND THE REST
OF THE WORLD

THIS YEAR YOU WILL

INCITE WONDER

**SO YOUR CHILD WILL KNOW GOD'S LOVE
AND MEET GOD'S FAMILY.**

Your one-year-old listens to your words. So this phase is the perfect time to begin talking, singing, and praying together with your toddler. Begin by simply incorporating faith into your daily routines.

SAY THINGS LIKE . . .

**GOD MADE YOU.
GOD LOVES YOU.
JESUS WANTS TO BE YOUR
FRIEND FOREVER.**

**GOD, THANK YOU FOR . . .
GOD, PLEASE HELP US . . .**
(Pray aloud while you are with your one-year-old.)

JESUS LOVES ME.
(Sing songs together.)

LET'S GO TO CHURCH!
(Connect with a faith community.)

Who will help you develop your child's faith as they grow?

Is there a volunteer at your church who shows up consistently each week for your child? Do you attend a consistent service so your kid knows who will greet them each week?

_____

_____

_____

_____

_____

_____

_____

_____

_____

_____

_____

_____

_____

_____

_____

_____

_____

_____

_____

_____

_____

_____

When it comes to your child's faith, what do you hope is true for them 884 weeks from now?

_____

_____

_____

_____

_____

_____

_____

_____

_____

_____

_____

_____

_____

_____

_____

_____

_____

_____

_____

What routines or habits do you have in your own life that are stretching your faith?

_____

_____

_____

_____

_____

_____

_____

_____

_____

_____

_____

_____

_____

_____

_____

_____

_____

_____

_____

_____

THE

OF YOUR

WEEK

—

WILL SHAPE

THE VALUES

IN YOUR

home.

NOW THAT YOU HAVE FILLED THIS BOOK WITH DREAMS, IDEAS, AND GOALS, IT MAY SEEM AS IF YOU WILL NEVER HAVE TIME TO GET IT ALL DONE.

Actually, you have *884 weeks*.

And every week has potential.

The secret to making the most of this phase with your one-year-old is to take advantage of the time you already have. Create a rhythm to your weeks by leveraging these four times together.

Set the mood for the day. Smile. Greet them with words of love.

Reinforce simple ideas. Talk to your toddler and play music as you go.

Be personal. Spend one-on-one time that communicates love and affection.

Wind down together. Provide comfort as the day draws to a close.

What seem to be your toddler's best times of the day?

_____

_____

_____

_____

_____

_____

_____

_____

_____

_____

_____

_____

_____

_____

_____

_____

_____

_____

_____

_____

_____

_____

_____

_____

What are some of your favorite routines with your toddler?

_____

_____

_____

_____

_____

_____

_____

_____

_____

_____

_____

_____

_____

_____

_____

_____

_____

_____

_____

_____

_____

_____

Write down any other thoughts or questions that you have about parenting your one-year-old.

_____

_____

_____

_____

_____

_____

_____

_____

_____

_____

_____

_____

_____

_____

_____

_____

_____

_____

_____

_____
_____
_____
_____
_____
_____
_____
_____
_____
_____
_____
_____
_____
_____
_____
_____
_____
_____
_____
_____
_____
_____
_____
_____

EVERY KID → MADE IN THE IMAGE OF GOD = *LOVE GOD*

Incite →
wonder

SO THEY WILL . . .
KNOW GOD'S LOVE
& MEET GOD'S FAMILY

Provoke →
discovery

SO THEY WILL . . .
TRUST GOD'S CHARACTER
& EXPERIENCE GOD'S FAMILY

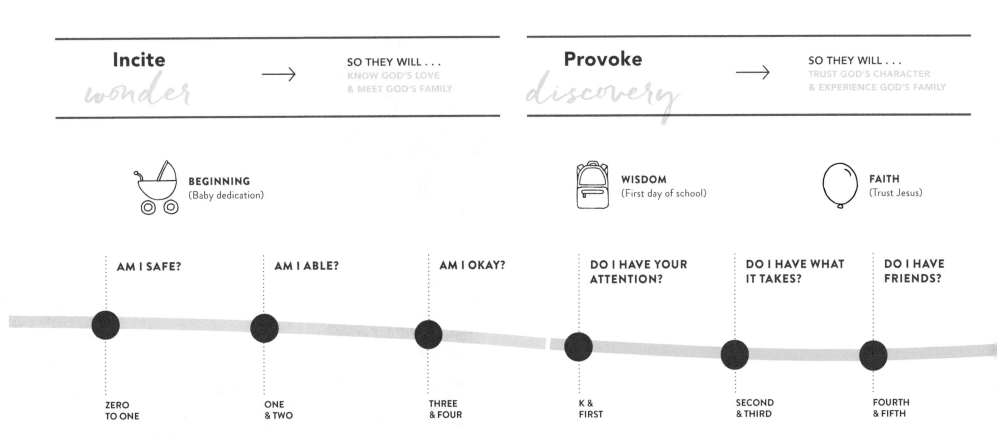

BEGINNING
(Baby dedication)

WISDOM
(First day of school)

FAITH
(Trust Jesus)

AM I SAFE?

AM I ABLE?

AM I OKAY?

DO I HAVE YOUR ATTENTION?

DO I HAVE WHAT IT TAKES?

DO I HAVE FRIENDS?

ZERO TO ONE

ONE & TWO

THREE & FOUR

K & FIRST

SECOND & THIRD

FOURTH & FIFTH

EMBRACE *their physical needs*

ENGAGE *their interests*

YOU HAVE

APPROXIMATELY

884 WEEKS.

WITH
ALL THEIR
HEART
SOUL
STRENGTH

AND

trust
Jesus

→

TO HAVE
A BETTER
FUTURE

Provoke
discovery →

SO THEY WILL . . .
OWN THEIR OWN FAITH
& VALUE A FAITH COMMUNITY

Fuel
passion →

SO THEY WILL . . .
KEEP PURSUING AUTHENTIC FAITH
& DISCOVER A PERSONAL MISSION

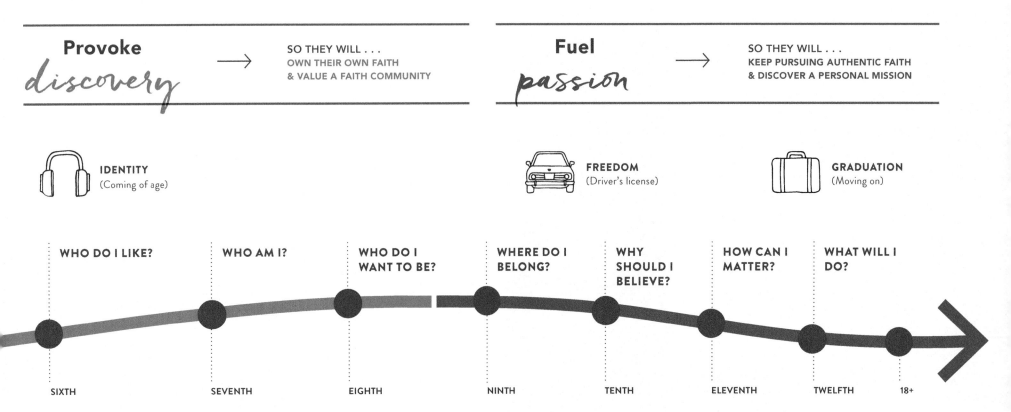

IDENTITY
(Coming of age)

FREEDOM
(Driver's license)

GRADUATION
(Moving on)

WHO DO I LIKE? | WHO AM I? | WHO DO I WANT TO BE? | WHERE DO I BELONG? | WHY SHOULD I BELIEVE? | HOW CAN I MATTER? | WHAT WILL I DO?

SIXTH | SEVENTH | EIGHTH | NINTH | TENTH | ELEVENTH | TWELFTH | 18+

AFFIRM their personal journey

MOBILIZE their potential

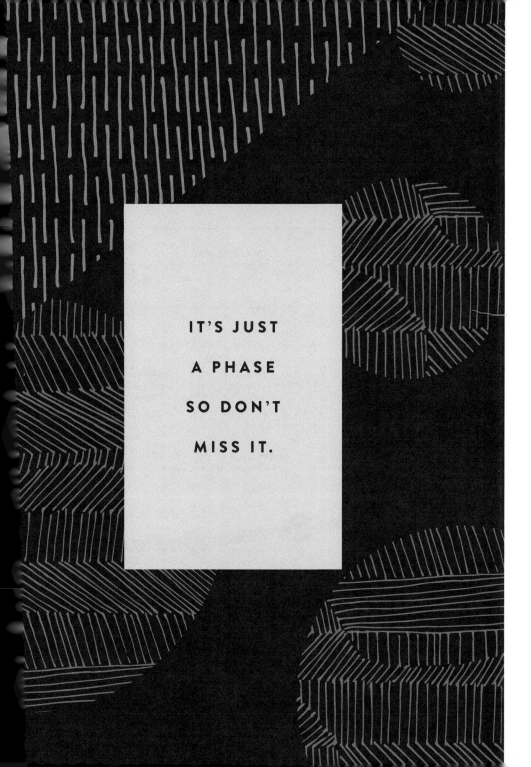

IT'S JUST
A PHASE
SO DON'T
MISS IT.

ABOUT THE AUTHORS

KRISTEN IVY @kristen_ivy

Kristen Ivy is executive director of the Phase Project. She and her husband, Matt, are in the preschool and elementary phases with three kids: Sawyer, Hensley, and Raleigh.

Kristen earned her Bachelors of Education from Baylor University in 2004 and received a Master of Divinity from Mercer University in 2009. She worked in the public school system as a high school biology and English teacher, where she learned firsthand the importance of influencing the next generation.

Kristen is also the executive director of messaging at Orange and has played an integral role in the development of the elementary, middle school, and high school curriculum and has shared her experiences at speaking events across the country. She is the co-author of *Playing for Keeps, Creating a Lead Small Culture, It's Just a Phase*, and *Don't Miss It*.

REGGIE JOINER @reggiejoiner

Reggie Joiner is founder and CEO of the reThink Group and co-founder of the Phase Project. He and his wife, Debbie, have reared four kids into adulthood. They now also have two grandchildren.

The reThink Group (also known as Orange) is a non-profit organization whose purpose is to influence those who influence the next generation. Orange provides resources and training for churches and organizations that create environments for parents, kids, and teenagers.

Before starting the reThink Group in 2006, Reggie was one of the founders of North Point Community Church. During his 11 years with Andy Stanley, Reggie was the executive director of family ministry, where he developed a new concept for relevant ministry to children, teenagers, and married adults. Reggie has authored and co-authored more than 10 books including: *Think Orange*, *Seven Practices of Effective Ministry*, *Parenting Beyond Your Capacity*, *Playing for Keeps*, *Lead Small*, *Creating a Lead Small Culture*, and his latest, *A New Kind of Leader* and *Don't Miss It*.

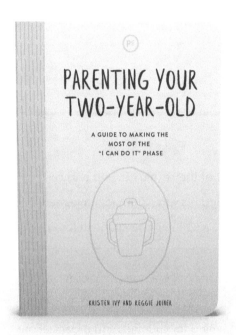

MAKE THE MOST OF EVERY PHASE IN YOUR CHILD'S LIFE

The guide in your hand is one of an eighteen-part series.

So, unless you've figured out a way to freeze time and keep your one-year-old from turning into a two-year-old, you might want to check out the next guide in this set.

Designed in partnership with Parent Cue, each guide will help you rediscover . . .

**what's changing about your kid,
the 6 things your kid needs most,
and 4 conversations to have each year.**

WANT TO GIFT A FRIEND WITH ALL 18 GUIDES
OR HAVE ALL THE GUIDES ON HAND FOR YOURSELF?

ORDER THE ENTIRE SERIES OF PHASE GUIDES TODAY.